IF YOU COULD MAKE FROGS...

For Mather, Owen, Lucy,
Adaline and Mason

Published in the U.S.A.

Fifth Edition - December 2018

ISBN: 9781977034960

IF YOU COULD MAKE
FROGS...

written by
GRANDPA PETE

illustrated by
ZACHARY PRESTON

Why do people have different color
skin and come in all kinds of sizes
and shapes?

That's the way God made us.
God is very creative!
Let's look at some other
things he made.

Do YoU HaVe a DoG?

We have a little brown dog called a Yorkie-Poo. Mason has a huge black dog called a German Shepherd. When I was a kid, we always had short red dogs called dachshunds.

Evan has a dog named smoochie!

Hmmmmm... why did God make so
many different kinds of dogs?

I guess because He could.

If you could make dogs, would
you make them all the same?
I wouldn't. That would be boring!

Fish come in all kinds of shapes,
sizes, and colors. Some live in
fresh water, some in salty water.

Some have big teeth,
some have shiny scales.

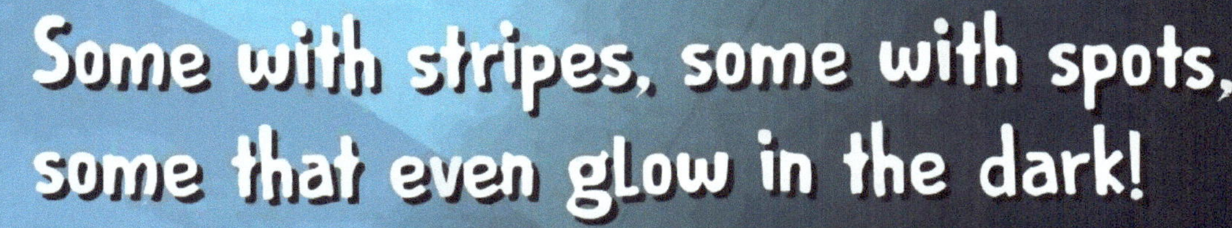

Some with stripes, some with spots,
some that even glow in the dark!

Fish are all different too.
God has a huge imagination so
He made a big variety.
Check these out!

Birds are amazing!

Little tiny humming birds zooming around like helicopters, bright yellow canaries and finches, red robins and cardinals, colorful toucans.

QUACK

ALL birds are different.
What a bLast!

This is my favorite.
God must have worked
hard on this one!

Even frogs come in different colors!

Blue with black spots, green with yellow and blue sides and orange eyes, even black and orange frogs.

I think God had fun making frogs, don't you?
If you could make frogs,
why would you make them all the same?
Ribbet!

I was at the park today and noticed that there was no other bike just like mine!

There was one that was the same color, but I have a cool bell!

Our yard is full of flowers.
Tulips and Crocus in the spring,
roses amd Lillies in summer.
No flower is better than the other,
just different.

People come in all kinds of shapes, sizes
and colors too.

Red and yellow, black and white and brown skin.
Blonde hair, brown hair, black hair, red hair.
Some with no hair at all. Tall People, short people.

God is creative and he made us all different!

If you could make people,
whouldn't you make us all different too?

God gave us a beautiful variety of things. Just like you are one of kind, so is everybody else!

So treat everybody the same way you would like to be treated!

The End

In "Who Built the Birdhouse?" Taylor asks a question about evolution. Grandpa Pete explains that everything made needs a maker. Evolution is a silly idea that just does not make any sense at all!

Who Built
the
Birdhouse?
written by Grandpa Pete
Illustrated by Dan Krawczynski